TAKING ACTION ON CLIMATE CHANGE

DEHYDRATED
Escalating Droughts

ALEX DAVID

New York

Published in 2020 by Cavendish Square Publishing, LLC
243 5th Avenue, Suite 136, New York, NY 10016

First Edition

Website: cavendishsq.com

Library of Congress Cataloging-in-Publication Data

Names: David, Alex, author.
Title: Dehydrated : escalating droughts / Alex David.
Description: First edition. | New York : Cavendish Square, 2020. |
Series: Taking action on climate change | Includes bibliographical references and index.
Identifiers: LCCN 2019011337 (print) | LCCN 2019012798 (ebook) |
ISBN 9781502652270 (ebook) | ISBN 9781502652263 (library bound) |
ISBN 9781502652256 (pbk.)
Subjects: LCSH: Droughts--Juvenile literature. | Climatic changes--Effect of human beings on--Juvenile literature. | Climate change mitigation--Juvenile literature. | Climatic changes--Government policy--Juvenile literature. | Hydrologic cycle--Juvenile literature.
Classification: LCC QC929.25 (ebook) |
LCC QC929.25 .D38 2020 (print) | DDC 551.57/73--dc23
LC record available at https://lccn.loc.gov/2019011337

Copy Editor: Nathan Heidelberger
Associate Art Director: Alan Sliwinski
Designer: Ginny Kemmerer
Production Coordinator: Karol Szymczuk
Photo Research: J8 Media

The photographs in this book are used by permission and through the courtesy of:
Cover, Guido Dingemans, De Eindredactie/Moment/Getty Images; p. 4 JEKESAI NJIKIZANA/AFP/Getty Images; p. 8 Jakob Polacsek/Moment/Getty Images; p. 14 Saskia Nowicki, Nancy Gladstone, Jacob Katuva, Heloise Greeff, Achut Manandhar, Geofrey Wekesa and Geofrey Mwania/The Water Module - Student Resource, School of Geography and the Environment, University of Oxford 2018 (https://upgro.files.wordpress.com/2018/03/water-module-studentresource-web.pdf)/File: Diagram of the water cycle including some human activity.pdf/Wikimedia Commons/CCA-SA 4.0 International; p. 21 Dorling Kindersley/Getty Images; p. 22 Ron Thomas/E+/Getty Images; p. 25 Intergovernmental Panel on Climate Change Documents and Website/File: Intergovernmental Panel on Climate Change Logo.svg/Wikimedia Commons/Public Domain; p. 26 The Asahi Shimbun/Getty Images; p. 31 Yvan Cohen/LightRocket/Getty Images; p. 33 trgrowth/Shutterstock.com; p. 34 TPG/Getty Images; p. 36 Carpodacus, Own work/File: Ancient irrigation system in Nurata.jpg/Wikimedia Commons/CCA-SA 4.0 International; p. 37 Jim West/Alamy Stock Photo; p. 39 STEPHANE DE SAKUTIN/AFP/Getty Images; p. 41 Mikkel Juul Jensen/Science Source; p. 42 Deon Raath/Foto24/Gallo Images/Getty Images; p. 44 Tebogo Letsie/City Press/Gallo Images/Getty Images; p. 47Donald Iain Smith/Photodisc/Getty Images; p. 49 Pack-Shot/Shutterstock.com; p. 50 ISAAC KASAMANI/AFP/Getty Images; p. 52 YASUYOSHI CHIBA/AFP/Getty Images.

Printed in the United States of America

Portions of this book originally appeared in *Adapting to Droughts* by Larry Gerber.

CONTENTS

These women in Zimbabwe are carrying boxes of porridge donated by the World Food Programme during a drought.

Introduction

Imagine your life without water. Imagine no food, no showers, no toilets, no swimming pools, and no clean water running from a tap. Imagine having to pack up your house. Imagine driving in a large truck away from everything you know. The dry desert surrounds you. Maybe your throat is parched. Maybe you are hungry. You are forced to leave your community to search for water.

A Real Nightmare

For people in parts of Africa, this was not an imagined nightmare, but reality. From 2005 to 2017, many parts of East Africa experienced extreme drought. In 2011, droughts in the Horn of

Africa were particularly severe. Lands became parched. Soil turned from moist and fertile to dry and void of nutrients. Over 12 million people were affected by the drought; 7.5 million people in Ethiopia alone needed food aid. Their farms dried up. Their livestock died. They packed up their homes and traveled in search of new areas that might have water. Children dropped out of school so that they could help their parents find water. Women bound rope around their bodies to try to avoid the feeling of starvation. All of this happened simply because it would not rain.

The lack of water caused conflict. People began to starve. In South Sudan and Somalia, people began to fight. Where there is no water, there is no peace.

Governments tried to help their people. The government in Kenya gave $208 million in aid. Ethiopia spent $47 million. Still, people were starving. They were forced to migrate in search of water.

Droughts Today

A drought is a lack of water or rainfall in an area. Droughts affect many parts of the world today. Some say droughts are becoming more common because of global warming and climate change—major problems of the twenty-first century.

Today, droughts are making news headlines more and more. Places where rain used to fall heavily now have dried up. For example, from 2011 to 2019, people in California were severely impacted by droughts. According to the National Integrated Drought Information System, since 2000, the longest period of drought in California lasted for 376 weeks. It started on December 27, 2011, and finally let up on March 5, 2019. Because of this unusually dry weather, trees became perfect kindling for forest fires. Drought helped to create perfect conditions for the deadliest fire in California's history to that point: the Camp Fire of 2018.

Acting Now

Drought requires people to rethink their relationship to water and take action. In areas where drought happens more and more, people can take action in a number of ways. First, it's good to be informed about the situation. With knowledge about changing weather patterns and causes of droughts, we can better address the situation in the future. Second, we can work toward developing better lifestyle habits and promote good habits in others. Third, we can try to enact change at a governmental and global level by getting politicians and activists involved. Taking these steps will also require adaptation and dedication. However, if we can achieve these goals, we can ensure a more stable, environmentally considerate future.

Rain pours over the Indian Ocean near Indonesia.

CHAPTER 1

The Cycle of Life

People have often felt powerless in determining whether or not rain will fall. They've created rituals and dances asking nature to send rain. Rain gods were popular in ancient communities too. Today, we know rain is part of the water cycle.

Through science, we can better understand why rain falls at some times and not at others. Rain is part of a delicate system that is affected by many factors. In the twenty-first century, some factors are leading to less rain and a terribly parched earth, sometimes creating desperate situations.

What Is Drought?

Drought is something that happens when normal rainfall does not occur. According to a 2016 article published in *Environmental Research Letters*, there is no universally accepted definition of drought because the impacts of drought depend on the region. Unlike hurricanes, which have a very clear start and end, droughts do not have a clear start and end. Drought simply means a shortage of water. However, climatologists have labeled four types of drought: meteorological droughts, hydrological droughts, agricultural droughts, and socioeconomic droughts.

Meteorological Droughts

Meteorological droughts occur when there are sustained dry weather patterns over a region. Meteorological droughts can begin and end quickly. They create hydrological and agricultural droughts.

Hydrological Droughts

Hydrological droughts occur when sources of water appear to be running low. This may include rivers, lakes, or reservoirs. Hydrological droughts mainly affect water-dependent operations, like power plants and irrigation. Sometimes there is a groundwater drought, which means that the water levels in subsurface storage areas are exceptionally low. A groundwater drought will reduce drinking water supply.

Agricultural Droughts

Agricultural droughts occur when there is not enough water for crops. The soil becomes dry, and there is not enough water to sustain plants. This kind of drought affects the food supply.

Socioeconomic Droughts

Occurring from all of the above droughts, socioeconomic droughts create financial loss. They are different from the other types of drought because they depend on supply and demand. Many economic goods rely on water: fish, hydroelectric power, and grains, for example. Socioeconomic drought occurs when a demand for a good exceeds supply. Therefore, a community might need hydroelectric power, but because power plants use water to produce electricity, the supply is limited. This community would be in a socioeconomic drought.

After understanding the various types of drought, it's easy to see how droughts can impact communities. However, we are still left questioning: Why doesn't it rain?

New Weather Patterns

Drought is a normal part of weather systems, but East Africa hadn't experienced such dry weather since the 1950s. However, some years it experienced higher than normal rainfall. This was seen in California as well. California's weather patterns shift continuously. Some years it has water and some years it doesn't. Scientists know that these increased droughts may have been caused by human-created climate change. Global warming has caused changes in climatic cycles. Weather patterns like El Niño, La Niña, and the Indian Ocean Dipole are intensifying because of global warming. Some areas are getting too much rain and flooding, while others are getting much less.

La Niña and El Niño

La Niña and El Niño occur in the tropical Pacific Ocean. They are opposite forces that are part of a natural climate pattern. La Niña is the cool phase, and El Niño is the warm phase. On average, every three to seven years, they swing back and forth, creating differences in ocean temperatures, winds, surface pressure, and rainfall.

When La Niña is in effect, the ocean current cools surface waters in the central and eastern Pacific Ocean, so that warmer water builds up in the western Pacific. When this happens, Australia and Indonesia get more rain than normal, and western winds strengthen over the Indian Ocean. These winds pull moisture away from eastern Africa. The result: drought, dead cattle and crops, and millions of thirsty and starving refugees.

When El Niño takes over, ocean temperatures in the central and eastern parts of the tropical Pacific Ocean become warmer than average. Indonesia gets less rain, while the central and eastern parts of the Pacific Ocean get more rain and increased rising air. This creates storms and rain. However, because of the sinking air over Indonesia, Indonesia becomes drier.

The Indian Ocean Dipole

Similar to El Niño is the Indian Ocean Dipole. It's so similar that it's actually sometimes called the Indian Niño. Researchers know less about this effect, as it was only discovered in 1999 by Japanese researchers. However, scientists do know that as the ocean warms, it evaporates more water. In the summer of 2016, the ocean was warmer by 1.8 degrees Fahrenheit (1 degree Celsius). A warmer ocean created more moisture in the air above the eastern Indian Ocean. Wind is a means of the atmosphere trying to equalize differences in density, pressure, and temperature, so strong winds began as the atmosphere reacted to the cool, moist air. A warm wind began to sweep east across African land and out into the ocean. Farmers in the Horn of Africa were severely impacted because they needed moisture from the Indian Ocean. They relied on the rains that usually came in October to December, and then later in March to June. The rain that was supposed to come in October was late and in some places never came at all. The lack of rain created famine and displaced many families.

Sources of Water

To understand drought, we must understand the scientific principle of the water cycle. When the sun warms the ocean's surface, water evaporates into the atmosphere, leaving the salt behind. As the water vapor rises, it cools and condenses, forming clouds that bring rain and snow. Some of this precipitation falls

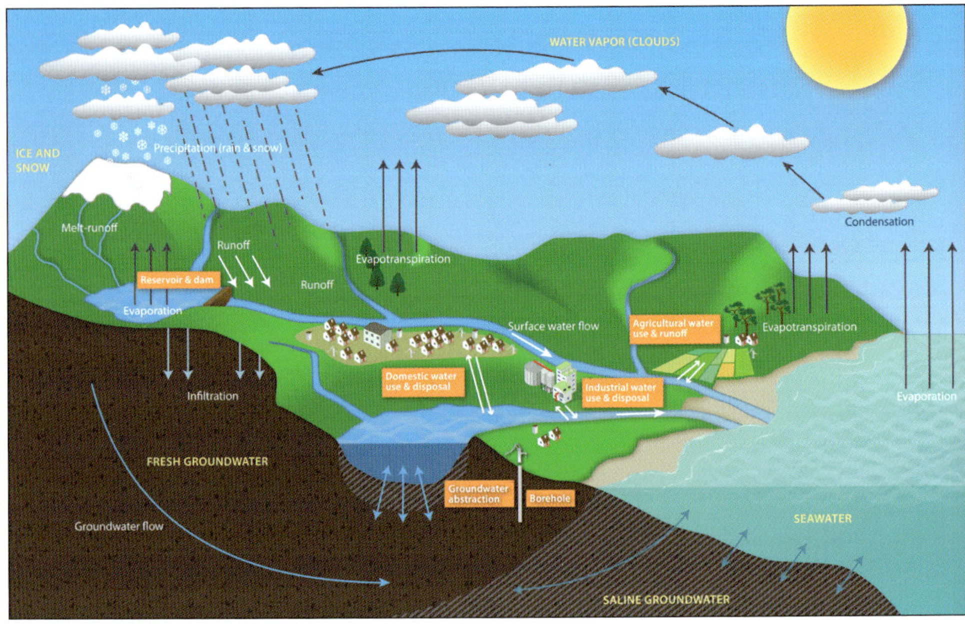

This is a diagram of the water cycle, which includes human activity.

on land and seeps beneath the ground, forming underground lakes called aquifers. Many communities get their water from wells drilled down into aquifers. However, many aquifers are being threatened.

One example is the state of Florida. In the twenty-first century, it has been booming with development. Houses, condos, and resorts are all being constructed for a thriving tourist market. This seems like a great thing for the economy, but for the water supply, it is a different story. A limestone aquifer, called the Floridan aquifer system, is burrowed under the state of Florida. It covers 100,000 square miles (259,000 square kilometers) and also extends under parts of Alabama, Georgia,

Mississippi, and South Carolina. On top of the Floridan aquifer is the Biscayne aquifer. These aquifers allow Floridians to get the clean water they use for everything from bathing and washing dishes to swimming and maintaining golf courses. However, so many people using the water is putting serious strain on the system. According to the Florida Springs Institute, the aquifers have dropped significantly in the past seventy-five years. The aquifers are below the level needed to supply these communities. Scientists predict that by 2035 there will not be enough water from the aquifers. New sources of water and lifestyle modification are needed. Florida residents may have to look for water from other places, such as reclaimed water or surface water.

The Delicate Cycle

Earth's water cycle is almost too huge to imagine, but it is also very delicate. We tend to think simplistically of the oceans as enormous basins of water. Actually, ocean water is constantly moving. Earth's seas are crisscrossed by currents, which are propelled by differences in water temperature and salinity, or saltiness. Currents move not only across ocean surfaces but also upward and downward, into and out of the ocean's depths. These currents are often compared to giant conveyor belts. They carry along warmer or cooler water, which affects air temperature and regulates weather over land as well as over the sea. These currents help determine whether or not it rains in a given region.

Short Supply

The world population is increasing year after year. The more it increases, the larger and more complicated the problem of global warming–related drought becomes. For one thing, it means there is less water to go around. In 1800, there were about 1 billion people on the planet; in 2018, there were 7.6 billion people. Every day, that number grows. However, the amount of the world's fresh water has stayed the same, and most of it isn't available to people.

A growing population also requires a growing food supply. Increasing the food supply means increasing water usage. It takes a lot of water to raise animals, grow crops, and process food. Increased farming strains water supplies because many important food crops need irrigation, and cattle and other livestock need water. When water becomes scarce, crops and livestock die. That means there is less food to go around, and the remaining food costs more. Meanwhile, farmers have been burning many of the world's remaining forests to clear land for the crops and animals necessary to increase the food supply for a hungry planet.

Fresh Water

Most of Earth's water supply is in the oceans and is too salty to drink. Only about 3 percent of Earth's water is fresh. That amount doesn't change much. It is constantly being naturally recycled

THE DUST BOWL DROUGHT OF THE 1930S

From the late 1800s until the 1930s, farmers began turning over the previously unplowed native grasses of the Great Plains to plant wheat and other crops. Life on the windy prairie was often hard, but with adequate rainfall, it was possible to make a living.

In 1931, however, the rains stopped. With the grass gone, there was nothing to hold the dirt in place. Huge wind storms—"black blizzards"—swept up tons of topsoil, making it difficult to breathe and causing lung diseases. As the drought continued, farmers went broke. Thousands packed up and moved away, most heading west to the still fertile valleys of California. This was the largest migration caused by a natural disaster in the nation's history.

Through his Soil Conservation Service, President Franklin D. Roosevelt began a program of planting trees and crops such as legumes and alfalfa. These and other measures helped rebuild the soil and prevent erosion.The drought continued until 1939, when it finally began to rain again. The so-called Dust Bowl years continue to be the worst drought in US history as of 2019.

but not increased. Of the total amount of this already limited supply of fresh water, only a fraction is in places where people and animals can access it. Most of it—about 68 percent—is frozen in glaciers and ice sheets; another 30 percent is underground and out of reach.

However, glaciers and ice sheets around the world have been disappearing faster than ever before recorded. Areas that relied on naturally melting glaciers now have less water in their reservoirs.

For instance, the South American country of Bolivia relies on glaciers in the Andes Mountains to bring water to the cities of La Paz and El Alto. In 2014, the glaciers nearly ran dry. NASA satellite imagery showed that the glaciers shrunk from 204 square miles (530 square kilometers) in 1986 to about 116 square miles (300 square kilometers) in 2014. This caused Bolivia to declare a state of emergency. It was the worst drought they had experienced in twenty-five years. As the glaciers disappeared, water could no longer flow into the three main dams that supply these cities. Bolivia took drastic steps to help tackle this problem. Armed forces distributed water, and residents were told to ration their water.

Bolivia's water problems didn't stop there. Another source of water in Bolivia, Lake Poopó, began to dry up. In 2018, this caused problems for indigenous people living there. Because the lake had diminished by that point, there were no longer any fish. The Uru people who used to make their living from the water now had to collect salt to sell it and earn a living. Although there are other factors besides global warming (like a nearby tin mine) that have caused the lake to dry up, rising temperatures have greatly impacted Bolivia's water crisis.

Droughts are equal-opportunity catastrophes. They strike both developing and developed countries. Germany suffered from the impact of drought in 2018. That year, high temperatures affected 90 percent of Germany for four months. It hadn't been that dry there from April to July since 1881. The drought put Germany at risk for forest fires and affected its agricultural economy. Because drought changed the composition of the soil, farmers were not able to produce as much food during that time. According to the German Farmers Association, in some areas 70 percent of farmers' grain crops were lost. Because the farmers didn't have enough feed for their cows, they ended up slaughtering them.

It wasn't just Germany that was affected in 2018. Drought also swept across Greece, Portugal, Spain, and Sweden.

Water Wars

When water and food become scarce, the risk of war and other conflicts increases. The Syrian civil war has lasted since 2011, and water may be partially to blame. In 2006, water shortages in Syria made people move from rural communities into cities, where they were marginalized. Syria sits in a region historically called the Fertile Crescent, meaning it has rich soil, but between 2003 and 2009, the Tigris-Euphrates Basin, which is composed of Turkey, Syria, Iraq, and western Iran, lost water faster than any other place in the world, except northern India. Bad water management and lack of rainfall caused 117 million acres (48 million hectares) of fresh water to vanish. In Iraq, tensions over water (and a lack of a strong government) caused people to assassinate water irrigation officials. In Syria, the previously mentioned migration led cities to be full of unemployed people who were angry. They began to revolt. In 2017, in Iraq, powerful groups started to use water as a means of controlling people. They distributed water to buy loyalty and to intimidate people into doing what they wanted them to do.

In India and Pakistan, mistrustful neighbors must share a dwindling supply of water from shrinking glaciers in the Himalayas. Both countries have booming populations, increasing the demand for a dwindling supply of water. In 2019, after a suicide bomber killed more than forty troops in India, the country said it would not share its water with Pakistan. India decided to divert water from eastern tributaries of the Indus River to its own residents and leave Pakistan without the water it needed. The Indus River is a large river that flows through both countries, and under a previous agreement that the World Bank created, the river is supposed to be shared by both India and Pakistan. It's clear from these examples and other situations like them that water is emerging as not only a source of life but also a source of power.

It seems water will continue to be a precious commodity, as the world is not getting any less thirsty. By 2050, water

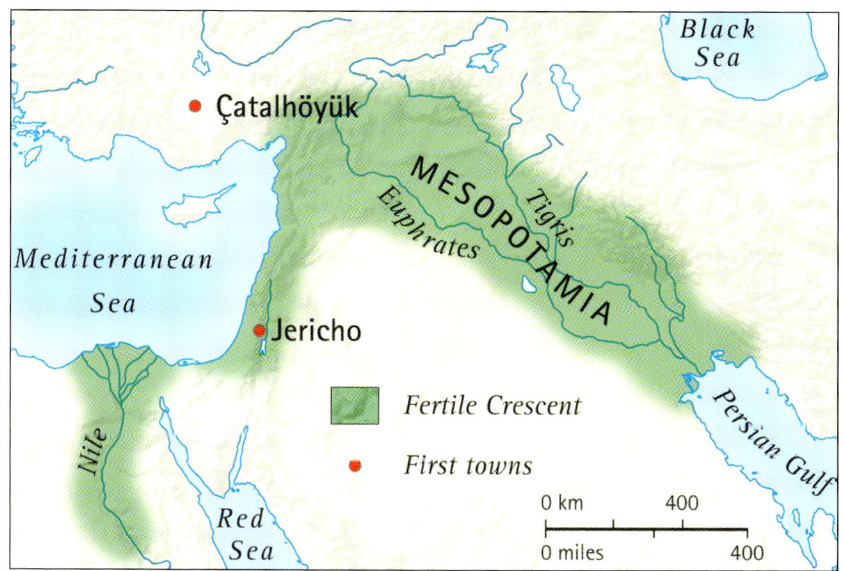

Above is a map of Fertile Crescent as it was in ancient times.

consumption is expected to increase by 55 percent. According to the Organization for Economic Cooperation and Development, by 2025, two-thirds of the world's population will be living in areas where water is scarce. Many experts worry that future wars will be fought over water—much as they have been fought over oil and other precious natural resources in the past—as politicians, big corporations, and thirsty people compete for a share of the shrinking global supply.

So, we can understand what drought is and the weather patterns that change rainfall. We can understand where fresh water is located and learn the tensions that are created when there isn't enough fresh water. However, to get to the root of the problem, we need to understand climate change, the reason why droughts are occurring more frequently.

Cars create carbon emissions in places all around the world, like this freeway in Los Angeles, California.

CHAPTER 2

Climate Change and Drought

In the book *Life of Pi*, a mirror hangs in a zoo with the words, "Do you know who the most dangerous animal in the zoo is?" written above it. Zoo goers perhaps expect the most dangerous animal to be a lion or a python, but instead they are confronted with their own reflection. This example rings true for global warming. Since 1950, Earth's temperature has risen higher than ever before in recorded history. Although nature is cyclical and natural climate changes have occurred previously, scientists agree that today's consistently higher temperatures have been caused largely by human industrialization. Drought is one of the by-products of a warming world.

Humans may be the most dangerous species, but they are also an inventive species that is making great efforts to reduce the impact of global warming and its resulting climate change. Most of these efforts are directed at eliminating or lowering the main cause of climate change—emissions of carbon dioxide and other greenhouse gases. The great majority of these gases come from the wealthy industrialized countries in North America, Europe, and Asia. The industrialized nations use most of the world's available energy and, as a result, produce the majority of carbon emissions. For this reason, much of the focus in the so-called developed world has been on reducing emissions from factories, cars, planes, and ships.

Climate Change History

The first major international conference on global warming and climate change was held in 1979. Participants called on all governments to try to slow down human-influenced climate change. In 1988, the United Nations set up the Intergovernmental Panel on Climate Change (IPCC) and ordered it to study and report on scientific findings from around the world. The IPCC is split into three working groups. The first group focuses on the physical science of climate change. The second group addresses adaptation strategies. The third group places emphasis on mitigation, or lessening the negative effects.

People have been studying atmospheric and climate changes in a scientific way for about two hundred years. After

This is the logo for the Intergovernmental Panel on Climate Change.

World War II, researchers began developing new instruments to record and transmit data on temperatures, atmospheric gases, winds, ocean currents, and other measurements, and they began placing these instruments all over the world—in the sky, land, ice, and oceans. They dug into the ocean floor, studied glaciers, and drilled into ice sheets for signs of past climate change. They developed new research methods such as carbon-14 testing to determine the age of things like ancient pollen and seeds. These provided clues to past variations in global climate.

The first computer models using some of this data were created in the 1950s. Scientists knew that global warming had taken place in the past and seemed to be occurring in the present. However, they weren't sure how fast it could happen or whether humans could cause it. In the following decades, evidence began mounting that the world's currently changing climate was being caused largely by the burning of fossil fuels. It was also observed that climatic shifts were occurring very rapidly—over the span of only a few decades or even years, rather than centuries or millennia, as in the past.

Earth Summit

People in many countries called for strong action, but not much was actually done. At the 1992 Earth Summit in Rio de Janeiro, Brazil, 154 countries signed the UN Framework Convention on Climate Change and agreed to take action against global warming. The conference set target goals for each country to reduce its greenhouse gas emissions. These targets were

Leaders met at the Earth Summit in Rio de Janeiro, Brazil, in 1992.

only voluntary, however, and many countries failed to meet the goals. At a follow-up conference in Kyoto, Japan, in 1997, most industrial countries made legally binding agreements to reduce their greenhouse emissions. US president Bill Clinton signed the treaty.

A year later, US oil companies, coal companies, and other major polluters joined in a multimillion-dollar campaign to persuade the public that the treaty was based on shaky scientific evidence. Under energy industry pressure, Congress failed to ratify the Kyoto Protocol, as it was called, and in 2001, President George W. Bush rejected it outright. He said it was too expensive and that it put an unfair burden on the United States because other big polluters like China and India were not required to reduce their emissions.

The Paris Agreement

In 2015, participating countries convened in Paris, France, for a summit to talk about climate change. Its goal was to reduce emissions and to keep global temperatures from increasing more than 3.6°F (2°C) above historical levels. The agreement reached at this summit was approved by 195 countries. Each strategized to reduce its dependence on gas-powered cars once the agreement's term started in 2020. One of the largest contributors to climate change, the United States, had originally signed the agreement, but in 2017, US president Donald Trump said the country would withdraw from it. As of 2019, it remained the only country not to commit.

Many in the United States were outraged at the decision to leave the Paris Climate Agreement and decided to take action at home instead. Scientists wrote letters, citizens marched, cities created their own climate change action plans, and in 2019, Representative Alexandria Ocasio-Cortez and Senator Ed Markey created what many think of as the building blocks of an environmental revolution: the Green New Deal. The Green New Deal hopes to take the vigor of Franklin Roosevelt's New Deal and apply it to the climate problems of today. It calls for the United States to reduce its carbon emissions. In cutting carbon, the Green New Deal hopes to create more jobs and boost the United States' economy. Critics of the plan say that its ambitions are impossible, but Ocasio-Cortez and Markey are hopeful they can get the measure to pass.

Taking Steps in South Korea

The IPCC held another conference in 2018 in South Korea to address climate change on a global level. One intention of the conference was to bring together information from researchers and scientists all over the world. These scholars presented their findings to the larger community so that they could identify where there were gaps in scientific research. The conference resulted in increased pressure for countries to reduce their carbon emissions. The IPCC found that "limiting global warming to 1.5°C

[2.7°F] would require rapid, far-reaching and unprecedented changes in all aspects of society." The conference stressed that urgent action is required and outlined a series of "mitigation pathways" that could be used across countries. The mitigation pathways include such responses as carbon dioxide removal, using renewable energies rather than coal, and reducing land used for agriculture.

Climate change is a difficult reality, but it also encourages intercultural communication and knowledge-sharing between countries so that humanity may face the crisis together. Collaboration and communication will prove to be the most effective ways of finding solutions. Without unity, little progress can be made in countries that contribute the most to climate change, and thus in the rest of the world.

The Science Behind the Greenhouse Effect

Scientists say humans are making Earth hotter by using gasoline, oil, coal, and other fossil fuels that release carbon dioxide into the atmosphere when burned. Carbon dioxide and other "greenhouse gases," such as methane and nitrous oxide, trap heat in the atmosphere, like glass windows trap heat inside a greenhouse. This natural process was first recognized in the 1800s, and scientists called it the "greenhouse effect."

Earth's atmosphere acts like the perfect blanket. It's just thin enough to let the sun's energy get through and warm the

INDIGENOUS PERSONS AND ECOSYSTEM RESTORATION

In February 2019, the Institute of Environmental Science and Technology at the Autonomous University of Barcelona (ICTA-UAB) found that ecological restoration projects that include indigenous persons are more successful than those that ignore traditional uses of land. Climate scientists typically have not fully utilized indigenous knowledge, but that is starting to change. According to Victoria Reyes-Garcia, a researcher at ICTA-UAB, "Indigenous peoples have taken leadership roles in restoring forests, lakes and rivers, grasslands and drylands, mangroves and reefs, and wetlands degraded by outsiders or climate change, successfully coupling the goals of restoration and increasing participation of local population."

Indigenous populations have better land-use practices. They often rotate cultivation systems, which sustains forest cover. They scatter hayseed and cull meadows to allow resilience in grasslands. They plant diverse seeds that keep soil fertile and use more effective waste management systems that allow soil to become carbon enriched. This study shows that traditional ways of interacting with our natural habitat are often overlooked and should perhaps be consulted and utilized more often.

In Malaysia, the Penan tribe uses traditional forest techniques in a region threatened by ecosystem destruction.

planet's surface. Yet it's also just thick enough to shield our planet from the full blast of solar radiation that would burn up all life. It's light enough to allow some of that solar radiation to bounce back into space after it reflects off the planet. Yet it's heavy enough to hold some of the reflected heat in place, so we don't freeze. The greenhouse effect has gotten a lot of bad press in the twenty-first century because of global warming, but life on Earth wouldn't be possible without it. The problem today is that we are adding more and more greenhouse gases to the atmosphere, where they are accumulating. This has changed the composition of the atmospheric blanket, making it heavier and denser with heat-trapping gases. As a result, the surface and ocean temperatures of Earth are rising.

Most climate experts believe these changes are already too extensive and too far advanced to halt or reverse. However, it's hoped that by reducing our output of greenhouse gases, we can slow down global warming before lots of negative cycles are triggered. Once they are triggered, life on Earth will become precarious due to increasing heat, mass extinctions, killer storms, rising ocean levels, severe floods, and catastrophic droughts.

Developing Countries and Drought

Those who suffer the most from drought are usually those who can least afford it—the subsistence farmers and herders who live in the world's poorest countries. People in these countries raise their own crops and cattle for personal use and consumption. When their crops and cattle die, they have nothing to eat and nowhere to turn.

Experts are constantly working on ways to help farmers and cattle herders make it through dry times. They include water-saving tools as well as drought-resistant crops. These tools and methods are designed to work in local conditions, and they vary from place to place.

The key words for most developing countries are "sustainable agriculture"—farming and ranching that can be continued indefinitely without depleting the natural resources that make them possible. Instead of cutting and burning forests for new fields or pastures, for example, farmers are encouraged to plant

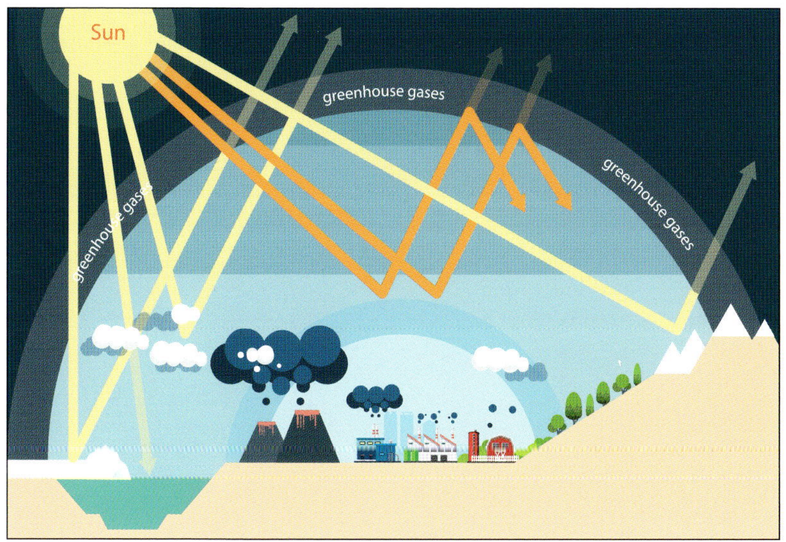

This is an illustration of the greenhouse effect.

trees. Tree leaves lock up the greenhouse gas carbon dioxide that would otherwise go into the atmosphere, and they emit oxygen. Tree roots hold moisture and soil in place, preventing heavy runoff of rainwater and soil erosion. They also provide a windbreak, preventing the blowing away of dry topsoil. Drought-resistant tree varieties, such as the moringa, offer other benefits. Known in India as the "miracle tree," the moringa has leaves and pods that can be eaten by humans and animals. Its seeds purify water, and its oil can be used to make soap. It can also be used for fuel and fertilizer.

It's clear that humans have created a global crisis. Rising temperatures have disastrous effects, including drought. As researchers and scientists seek solutions about our changing climate, they continually recommend that humans use mitigation to adjust to changing water supplies.

In 2018, China used a process called cloud seeding in an attempt to create rain.

CHAPTER 3

Mitigation

Mitigation means making something less painful or less dire. Researchers continually recommend that communities find ways to mitigate the effects of drought. The most obvious way to mitigate drought is to find more sources of fresh water, but this is not the only way.

New Sources of Water

Throughout human history, drought mitigation efforts have worked pretty well. People either found new sources of fresh water or figured out how to move water over considerable distances from existing sources to places where it was most needed. This approach usually involved digging wells or building dams, canals, ditches, aqueducts, or pipelines.

This is an example of an ancient irrigation project.

Water projects are as old as civilization. In fact, historians believe that the first civilizations developed in the Middle East when people began to cooperate on the construction and maintenance of the canals and ditches that irrigated their crops. The need for a single leader to coordinate this work may have led to the rise of early kings.

Modern cities and industrial areas could not exist without giant water projects. Southern California is an example. Much of the region is a desert. A little over one hundred years ago, officials estimated that the growing city of Los Angeles had enough water to support 250,000 people at most. If people kept moving in, the city would need more water. In 1913, Los Angeles completed an aqueduct, bringing water from California's Owens Valley, 250 miles (402 kilometers) to the north. The city later made deals to receive diverted water from the Colorado River and other sources. As more water became available to the city, more people moved there, and demand for water continued to grow. According to Erik Porse and other researchers, Los Angeles brings in 55 to 60 percent of its yearly water supply from outside sources.

Technological Mitigation Solutions

Earth's drinkable fresh water is just a tiny fraction of its total water supply. How can more of it be accessed and delivered to

The Los Angeles Aqueduct, shown here, brings water from the Owens Valley to Southern California.

RESURRECTION PLANTS

South African researcher Jill Farrant displays her resurrection plants.

In 2015, in a lab in South Africa, researcher Jill Farrant studied how plants survive during times of drought. She investigated the 130 types of resurrection plants, a type of flora that manages to survive when there is a shortage of water. Then, when rain falls again, the plants come completely back to life. In her lab, Farrant showed how these plants, which look dry and dead, quickly come back to life when given a drink of water.

By the end of 2030, climate change could completely dry out many parts of Africa. Farrant is studying the genetic code of resurrection plants in order to find ways to allow farmers to continue to grow crops in times of crisis. By looking at the teff plant, a type of cereal found in Ethiopia, she is hoping to activate genes in it that will allow it to survive droughts.

communities? Through the ages, humans have tried to answer this question by diverting and storing fresh water with the help of technology—wells, dams, canals, aqueducts, and pipelines. In the past one hundred years or so, however, people have invented new ways to tap into the water cycle itself, going directly to the ocean and the sky to test their ideas. Two of these methods are desalination and cloud seeding.

Desalination is a process by which salt is removed from seawater. Cloud seeding involves the use of airplanes or other means to disperse chemicals—usually silver iodide, dry ice, or salt—into the air. These chemicals can cause cloud condensation or the formation of ice crystals, which can then encourage increased precipitation. In theory, both methods of tapping into new fresh water sources sound great, but each has serious drawbacks.

Desalination

Desalination occurs naturally as part of the water cycle. When water evaporates from the surface of the ocean, it leaves behind salt. For a long time, people have known how to mimic this natural process using a method called distillation. If seawater is heated in a container, then allowed to cool and condense, salt and other impurities are removed. One major problem with distillation is that it takes energy of some sort to heat the water. Fuel can be expensive. If fossil fuels are burned to create the heat, the process creates carbon dioxide emissions and other forms of pollution. Another desalination method is osmosis: forcing the water through a thin surface that takes out the salt. However, most methods of osmosis require strong pressure to force the water through, and building up this pressure takes electricity. The energy needed is expensive, and generating it causes pollution.

Cloud Seeding

There are several methods of cloud seeding. Probably the best-known technique is to drop dry ice or silver iodide particles from an airplane into clouds. Without seeding, rainfall occurs when water naturally forms ice crystals near the top of storm clouds. With seeding, the silver iodide or dry ice promotes the formation of ice crystals, making it more likely that rain will fall. This method is called static cloud seeding. Using another method, hygroscopic cloud seeding, gunners on the ground shoot explosive shells full of salts into the lower parts of clouds. The tiny salt particles promote formation of more and bigger raindrops. Like desalination, however, cloud seeding is expensive, and there is disagreement about how well it works.

Even these advanced methods can no longer keep up with the growth of the world's population. If we are looking for ways to respond to drought, we have to keep looking for new, more effective, and practical solutions.

In addition to making droughts less severe and painful, humans must also learn to adapt. In fact, some motivated individuals are viewing droughts not as a cause for devastated

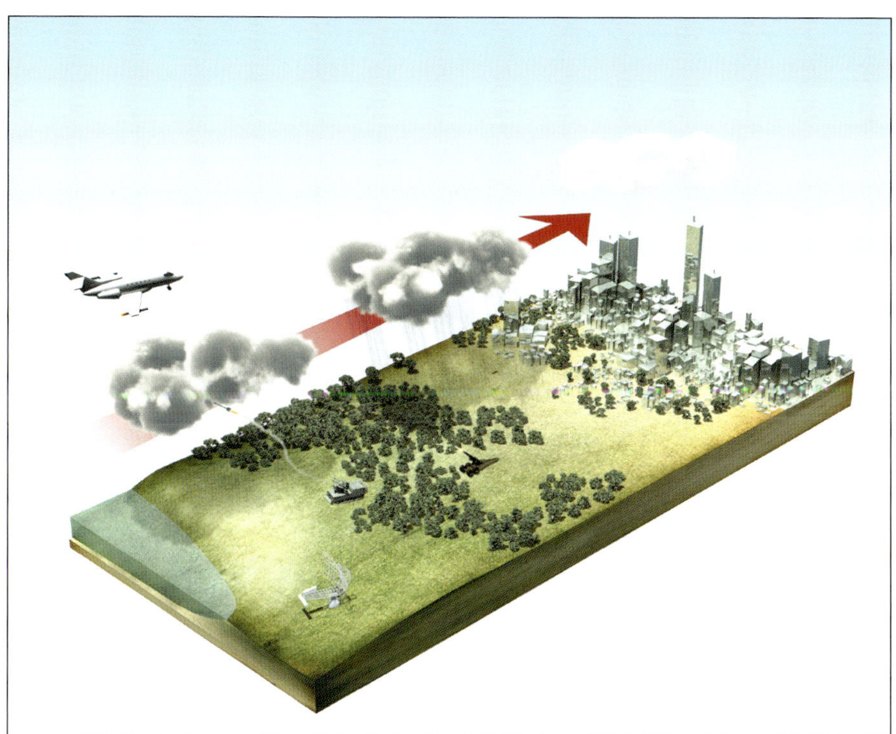

This is an illustration of cloud seeding: a plane "seeds" the clouds with silver iodide in an attempt to create rain.

hopelessness but rather as an opportunity for new ideas and new solutions.

Kiara Nirghin is one young woman who is creating new solutions to help with the effects of drought.

CHAPTER 4

New Solutions to New Problems

Researchers, scientists, engineers, and even young people like you are designing new machines, new technologies, new architecture, and new infrastructure that will assuage the problems of drought. All of these new ideas are being tried and tested to see what may help humans stay hydrated and tackle drought around the world.

Super Absorbent Polymer (SAP)

In 2016, Kiara Nirghin, a young woman from South Africa, created an ingenious invention: a polymer that stores water made from a mixture of orange peel and avocado skin. Nirghin was only sixteen years old! She was responding to the 2016 South African drought that affected thousands of communities, including her own. There wasn't enough water, and eight of the nine provinces were in a state of emergency. Nirghin won Google Science Fair's Community Impact Award for the Middle East and Africa.

Her invention could store water so that farmers could use it on their crops. It is called a super absorbent polymer because it is able to store an amount of water that weighs one hundred times more than it does. Additionally, it's made from discarded fruit, so it's reusing biodegradable material. Inventions like this show that creativity and innovation—even from young inventors—go a long way in fighting drought.

During droughts, cattle suffer.

Reusing Water

Recycling water is the focus of many drought adaptation plans. New, eco-friendly "smart homes" are equipped to save water and energy in many ways. They capture recycled, or "gray," water that would otherwise go down the drain. This includes water that has been used in sinks, bathtubs, and appliances like washing machines. Gray water cannot be used for drinking or bathing, but it is clean enough to be safe for many other uses. In particular, it can be used to flush toilets and water lawns, situations where drinkable water isn't needed. Using gray water thus lowers the demand for fully treated tap water.

Not all measures have to be high-tech or expensive. Many people are making personal "rain harvesting" systems using their own roofs. When it rains, water flows into gutters along the edges of the roof and into storage tanks or rain barrels. The rainwater is then saved and stored in the tanks for later use.

Modern Solutions

Since crop irrigation is one of the main uses of fresh water, many experts are concentrating on finding ways to help farmers make every drop count. Farmers struggled with drought long before global warming began, so some of these water-saving methods have been around a long time. They include drip irrigation and underground irrigation. These methods use small pipes and hoses to leak moisture directly onto the roots of crops, rather than spraying from above on the plants themselves.

DRAGGING ICEBERGS

One of the craziest-sounding drought-fighting ideas might not be as goofy as it first appears. In Antarctica, each year, the amount of smaller icebergs that calve, or break off, from larger ice sheets is greater than the amount of fresh water that is consumed globally. For some time, people have been talking about attaching cables to these fallen icebergs in the Arctic or Antarctic and towing them to thirsty regions. This idea surfaced in the 1940s, 1970s, and now in the twenty-first century. However, while there are iceberg-towing companies working over short distances in the Atlantic Ocean already, long-haul journeys have so far been only ideas, not yet reality.

In 2018, Nick Sloane, a marine salvage expert, proposed towing an iceberg from Antarctica to Cape Town, South Africa, a distance of over 4,000 miles (over 6,400 km). Cape Town was in a severe water shortage. It had built desalination plants and asked people to only flush toilets when necessary. However, these measures weren't enough. Moving an iceberg could solve water shortages, at least for a while. The one that was considered for Cape Town, for example, could have provided 40 million gallons (151 million liters) of fresh water per day for a year. To get the water from an iceberg, people would need to use a milling machine to create ice slurry to allow the water to be usable.

Towing icebergs to drought-affected areas is one of many mitigation strategies being considered as dry conditions become more common.

However, such a project, if carried out, would not be cheap. The Cape Town project would have cost $100 million, and it would have taken three months for the iceberg to arrive. People are skeptical such a tow could work, and they list several concerns regarding carrying out such a plan, including how much fuel towing vessels would use up on a journey that long. Rather than helping the planet, it could end up hurting it more.

Water that is applied to the roots directly is not wasted, whereas most of the water sprayed from above lands on leaves and evaporates. Another drought mitigation measure is to plant crops that are native to dry climates. These crops tend to be naturally drought-resistant and don't need nearly as much water to thrive.

Adaptation

In addition to making drought less painful, adaptation, or changing our habits, is essential. In order to survive, sometimes species need to make changes in their behavior. Strategies of adaptation allow humans to change the way they interact with droughts so that they are able to survive them.

Changing Infrastructure

We mentioned previously a type of drought called socioeconomic drought, which occurs when the demand outweighs the supply. However, there are times when rainfall increases and the supply of water actually outweighs the demand. If communities could build more groundwater storage spaces to collect this extra water, then they could use it when they found themselves in times of drought. This could include building infrastructure like percolation basins and injection walls.

Water and Electricity

Another strategy to reduce water consumption is to provide reclaimed water to power plants that use closed loop water

A home in France collects water in rain barrels.

circulation systems. Similar to the gray water strategy for some uses at home, local power plants don't need clean water and could instead use water that has been reclaimed.

As citizens, communities, and governments change the way they use water, they are preparing themselves for drought prevention. People realize that the cost of drought is too high and that further change needs to happen. This is why scientists and researchers from countries all over the world are getting together to discuss their findings on climate change. In doing so, they are trying to reduce the impact and occurrence of droughts. However, it's not just large government organizations that can create change. Youth movements are happening all around the world. You, too, can get involved and make a difference.

Students in Uganda protest climate change in order to inspire world leaders to act responsibly.

CHAPTER 5

You and Your World

As individuals, it may seem frustrating to live in a world where there is so much water and yet also encounter drought. People may feel powerless at times, but making even the smallest changes could bring huge results. If individuals gather together and change how they think and act, they can battle the droughts and climate change threatening today's world. More than ever before, young people around the world are speaking up about climate change because they are, rightly, concerned for the future of the planet.

Vanessa Nakate

In 2019, Vanessa Nakate, a college graduate from Uganda, took on the fight for climate change after seeing Greta Thunberg, a young activist from Sweden, protesting coal usage at COP24 (the United Nations Climate Conference that was held in Poland). Nakate was concerned for Uganda's water supply, as her country was at risk for desertification as a result of droughts. Desertification is when fertile fields turn into deserts because there is not enough water. After hearing Thunberg, Nakate realized that there were not enough activists in Africa who were speaking out. Nakate wanted to inform people about the dangerous effects of climate change. She often posted photos of herself to social media, showing her carrying a sign that read, "Green Love, Green Peace; Beat Plastic, Polythene, Pollution; Climate Strike Now."

Beatrice Phiri

In addition to protesting, spreading information about climate change is a powerful tool in fixing the crisis. Beatrice Phiri, a young person in Zambia, Africa, is using radio to do exactly this. Reacting to the changing weather patterns in Zambia, where it no longer rains as much as it used to, Phiri founded a nongovernmental organization (NGO) called Visionary Youth for Change in 2017. Phiri believes that changing people's mindsets is the key to protecting the environment. In her radio program, she goes to places dealing with environmental issues, like places where deforestation is occurring, and interviews community members. Her work in radio highlights the power of thoughtful, informed dialogue.

Conserve and Act

According to a 2018 study by the US Geological Survey, Americans are using less water than in the 1980s. On average, Americans have reduced their water consumption from 112 gallons (424 liters) to 82 gallons (310 L) per day.

By comparison, Germans use only about 51 gallons (193 L) per person per day; people in India use about 36 gallons (136 L); and people in China use 23 gallons (87 L). In the poorest countries, such as Haiti and Ethiopia, people get by on about 3 gallons (11 L) a day. Many ordinary citizens are calling on developed countries to use less water.

A sign in South Africa warns people that recycled water is not for drinking.

Everyone Deserves Water

Since 2010, the United Nations has recognized access to clean water as a basic human right. That doesn't mean everyone has a right to free water, but it does mean that governments should make sure everyone has equal access to affordable, safe drinking water. It also means that people who need water for drinking and washing take priority over other water users, such as industries.

The United Nations can't change water laws within individual states and countries, however. In the United States, companies, individuals, and governments are free to own, buy, sell—and dispute—water rights. An agreement struck in 1922, for example, divides the water of the Colorado River among eight western

In Mozambique, children carry empty water containers to collect water in 2019.

US states. Mexico, at the end of the line where the river flows into the sea, wasn't included in the agreement.

Climate change and drought are huge issues, and it takes huge steps to deal with them. Individual actions can help, of course, but since the problems were caused by entire societies, it stands to reason that all of society must seek, find, and put into practice a solution. There are many organizations dedicated to transforming the way society approaches the environment and humanity's impact upon it. They primarily strive to reduce greenhouse emissions, slow global warming, and adapt to the negative effects of both, including drought. In doing so, they use a variety of methods.

Global climate change is exactly that: global. It affects all of the countries in the world, but it does not affect them equally. More vulnerable countries and communities are more likely to suffer from the effects of drought. It is each person's responsibility to rethink their relationship to our resources. Rather than always valuing money over the environment, we need to see that water is as valuable as a monetary currency. It is our lifeblood, and we need to collaborate with one another to create positive, long-lasting change for future generations. We are the stewards of this earth, not the owners.

WOMEN FARMERS

In 2017, Paul Hawken edited a book called *Drawdown: The Most Comprehensive Plan Ever Proposed to Reverse Global Warming*. One part of the plan is to assist and educate young girls and women in low-income countries so that they may become farmers who are equal to their male counterparts. Although countries do not often break landowning statistics down by gender, it can be estimated that only 10 to 20 percent of landholders in developing countries are women. In many of these countries, women are legally prevented from owning their own land.

In low-income countries, women are just as competent farmers as men, but they lack the resources and funding to produce more food. Hawken states, "If all women smallholders receive equal access to productive resources, their farm yields will rise by 20 to 30 percent; 100 to 150 million people will no longer be hungry." By supporting women who are farmers, carbon emissions would lessen, because where there are profitable farms, there is less pressure to deforest the land. Alternating regenerative crops would also mean creating soil that is able to store carbon. Thus, by giving women farmers access to more funding, which could be used to buy farm tools, seeds, water, and other supplies needed to run a farm, not only will agriculture increase but carbon emissions will also decrease. Hawken's prediction is that if women who farmed 98 million acres (40 million ha) were to receive necessary assistance, 2.1 gigatons (2.3 billion US tons) of carbon dioxide could be reduced by 2050.

Glossary

aqueduct A channel for carrying water, usually built above ground and made of bricks, concrete, or stone.

aquifer A bed of porous rock that holds water.

desertification The process where fertile land becomes a desert.

distill To purify a liquid by first vaporizing it and then condensing it.

emission Something that is produced and sent or released into the open.

famine An extreme shortage of food.

gigaton A unit of measurement equal to 1 billion metric tons (1.1 billion US tons).

gray water Water collected from sinks, bathtubs, and other sources. It can be reused to water lawns and flush toilets, but it isn't clean enough to drink.

impurity A pollutant.

mitigate To make less painful.

osmosis The tendency of liquids to pass through a thin, permeable surface from a less concentrated solution to a more concentrated one.

polymer A substance with a molecular structure that is almost entirely bonded by similar units.

reservoir A basin for holding and storing water, usually created by damming a river.

slurry A semiliquid mixture.

Further Information

Books

Robinson, Mary. *Climate Justice: Hope, Resilience, and the Fight for a Sustainable Future*. New York, NY: Bloomsbury Publishing, 2018.

Rush, Elizabeth. *Rising: Dispatches from the New American Shore*. Minneapolis, MN: Milkweed Editions, 2019.

Shea, Therese. *Droughts and Heat Waves*. New York, NY: PowerKids Press, 2019.

Steele, Philip. *Analyzing Climate Change: Asking Questions, Evaluating Evidence, and Designing Solutions*. New York, NY: Cavendish Square, 2019.

Tillman, Ned. *The Big Melt*. Columbia, MD: South Branch Press, 2018.

Websites

Global Drought Information System
https://www.drought.gov/gdm/current-conditions
The Global Drought Information System monitors the world's drought situation.

US Drought Monitor
https://droughtmonitor.unl.edu
The drought monitor updates daily to show where droughts in the United States are.

The Water Project
https://thewaterproject.org/water_conservation
This site investigates water scarcity and shares water facts.

Organizations

American Water Works Association (AWWA)
6666 W. Quincy Ave.
Denver, CO 80235 USA
(303) 794-7711
Website: https://www.awwa.org
The AWWA is a scientific and educational nonprofit that provides information, opportunities for advocacy, and a network of water management resources.

Building Partnerships for Development (BPD) in Water and Sanitation
47-49 Durham Street
London, SE11 5JD
United Kingdom
+44 (0) 20 7793 4557
Website: http://www.bpdws.org/
The BPD aims to provide clean water to places in need by partnering with other organizations.

National Drought Mitigation Center (NDMC)
University of Nebraska–Lincoln
3310 Holdrege Street
P.O. Box 830988
Lincoln, NE 68583-0988
(402) 472-6707
Website: https://drought.unl.edu/Home.aspx
The NDMC conducts research and provides information on how people can prepare for drought and manage its risks.

Selected Bibliography

"Drought in East Africa: 'If the Rains Do Not Come, None of Us Will Survive.'" Oxfam International. Accessed February 20, 2019. https://www.oxfam.org/en/famine-and-hunger-crisis-ethiopia-food-crisis/drought-east-africa-if-rains-do-not-come-none-us-will.

Hawken, Paul. *Drawdown: The Most Comprehensive Plan Ever Proposed to Reverse Global Warming*. New York, NY: Penguin Books, 2018.

"Ice, Snow, and Glaciers: The Water Cycle." USGS Water Science School. Accessed March 1, 2019. https://water.usgs.gov/edu/watercycleice.html.

Karlsruhe Institute of Technology. "Drought Affected About 90% of German Territory in 2018." Phys.org, September 18, 2018. https://phys.org/news/2018-09-drought-affected-german-territory.html.

Knight, Bob. "Beyond Significant Harm." Florida Springs Institute, February 13, 2019. https://floridaspringsinstitute.org/beyond-significant-harm.

Mercado, Angely. "Uganda's Young Climate Activists Are Going on Strike." *Nation*, March 14, 2019. https://www.thenation.com/article/ugandas-young-climate-activists-are-going-on-strike.

Monks, Kieron. "16-Year-Old South African Invents Wonder Material to Fight Drought." CNN, August 14, 2016. https://www.cnn.com/2016/08/09/africa/orange-drought-kiara-nirghin/index.html.

Porse, Erik, Kathryn B. Mika, Elizaveta Litvak, Kimberly F. Manago, Terri S. Hogue, Mark Gold, Diane E. Pataki, and Stephanie Pincetl. "The Economic Value of Local Water Supplies in Los Angeles." *Nature Sustainability* 1, no. 6 (2018): 289–297. doi:10.1038/s41893-018-0068-2.

Progress Report: International Conference on Climate Change and Cities. Incheon, South Korea: IPCC, October 1–5, 2018. https://www.ipcc.ch/site/assets/uploads/2018/12/100920181041-INF1Rev1CitiesReport.pdf.

Rosenblum, Mort, and Doug Williamson. *Squandering Eden: Africa at the Edge*. Orlando, FL: Harcourt Brace Jovanovich, 1987.

"SA Scientist Using 'Resurrection Plants' to Battle Drought." News24, November 22, 2015. https://www.news24.com/Green/News/sa-scientist-using-resurrection-plants-to-battle-drought-20151122.

"Science and Politics of Climate Change." *New York Times*, December 12, 2009. http://www.nytimes.com/interactive/2009/12/07/science/20091207_CLIMATE_TIMELINE.html

Smedley, Tim. "Is the World Running Out of Fresh Water?" BBC News, April 12, 2017. http://www.bbc.com/future/story/20170412-is-the-world-running-out-of-fresh-water.

"This 20-Year-Old Zambian Is Determined to Fight Climate Change." *Marie Claire*, June 21, 2018. http://www.marieclaire.co.za/mc-recommends/beatrice-phiri-interview.

Universitat Autonoma de Barcelona. "Indigenous Knowledge, Key to a Successful Ecosystem Restoration." *ScienceDaily*, February 26, 2019. https://www.sciencedaily.com/releases/2019/02/190226112300.htm.

"Working Group II: Impacts, Adaptation and Vulnerability." Intergovernmtenal Panel on Climate Change. Accessed March 1, 2019. https://www.ipcc.ch/working-group/wg2.

Index

About the Author

Alex David has her MFA from New England State College. She has written a series of books called *We the Weirdos*. Her poems and short stories have been published in literary journals such as *Green Mountains Review* and *Adelaide Literary Magazine*. Additionally, she has taught a class on eco-fiction at Canisius College in Buffalo, New York. She loves to learn and write about climate science. She is hopeful for the future.